The Christmas Day Kitten

James Herriot

Illustrated by Ruth Brown

Piper Books

Christmas can never go by without my remembering a certain little cat. I first saw her when I called to see one of Mrs Pickering's much-loved Basset hounds.

I looked in some surprise at the furry creature moving quietly down the hall.

'I didn't know you had a cat,' I said to Mrs Pickering, who was a plumpish, pleasant-faced woman.

Mrs Pickering smiled. 'We haven't really. Debbie is a stray. She comes here two or three times a week and we give her some food. I don't know where she lives.'

'Do you ever get the feeling that she wants to stay with you?' I asked.

'No.' Mrs Pickering shook her head. 'She's a timid little thing. Just creeps in, has some food, then slips away. She doesn't seem to want to let me help her in any way.'

I looked at the little tabby cat again. 'But she isn't just having food today.'

'It's a funny thing, but every now and again she pops through into the sitting-room and sits by the fire for a few minutes. It's as though she was giving herself a treat.'

The little cat was sitting very upright on the thick rug which lay in front of the fireplace in which the coals glowed and flamed. The three Bassets were already lying there but they seemed used to Debbie because two of them sniffed her in a bored manner and the third merely cocked a sleepy eye at her before flopping back to sleep.

Debbie made no effort to curl up or wash herself or do anything other than gaze quietly ahead. This was obviously a special event in her life, a treat.

Then suddenly she turned and crept from the room without a sound, and was gone.

'That's just the way it is with Debbie,' said Mrs Pickering, laughing. 'She never stays more than ten minutes or so, then she's off.'

I often visited the Pickering home and I always looked out for the little cat. On one occasion I spotted her nibbling daintily from a saucer at the kitchen door. As I watched, she turned and almost floated on light footsteps into the hall, then through into the sitting-room.

Debbie settled herself in the middle of the pile of Basset hounds in her usual way: upright, still, and gazing into the glowing fire.

This time, I tried to make friends with her but she leaned away as I stretched out my hand. However, I talked to her softly and I managed to stroke her cheek with one finger.

Then it was time for her to go and, once outside the house, she jumped up on to the stone wall and down the other side. The last I saw was the little tabby figure flitting away across the grassy field.

'I wonder where she goes?' I murmured.

'That's something we've never been able to find out,' said Mrs Pickering.

It was three months later that I next heard from Mrs Pickering – and it happened to be Christmas morning.

'I'm so sorry to bother you today of all days,' said Mrs Pickering apologetically.

'Don't worry at all,' I said. 'Which of the dogs needs attention?'

'It's not the dogs. It's … Debbie. She's come to the house and there's something very wrong. Please come quickly.'

I drove through the empty market square. The snow was thick on the road and on the roofs of the surrounding houses. The shops were closed but the pretty coloured lights of the Christmas trees winked in the windows.

Mrs Pickering's house was beautifully decorated with
tinsel and holly, and the rich smell of turkey and sage
and onion stuffing wafted from the kitchen. But she had a
very worried look on her face as she led me through to the
sitting-room.

Debbie was there, but she wasn't sitting upright in her
usual position. She was lying quite still – and huddled
close to her lay a tiny kitten.

I looked down in amazement. 'What have we got here?'

'It's the strangest thing,' Mrs Pickering replied. 'I haven't seen her for several weeks and then she came in about two hours ago, staggered into the kitchen, and she was carrying the kitten in her mouth. She brought it in here and laid it on the rug. Almost immediately I could see that she wasn't well. Then she lay down like this and she hasn't moved since.

I knelt on the rug and passed my hand over Debbie's body which Mrs Pickering had placed on a piece of sheet. She was very, very thin and her coat was dirty. I knew that she didn't have long to live.

'Is she ill, Mr Herriot?' asked Mrs Pickering in a trembling voice.

'Yes … yes, I'm afraid so. But I don't think she is in any pain.'

Mrs Pickering looked at me and I saw there were tears in her eyes. Then she knelt beside Debbie and stroked the cat's head while the tears fell on the dirty fur.

'Oh, the poor little thing! I should have done more for her.'

I spoke gently. 'Nobody could have done more than you. Nobody could have been kinder. And see, she has brought her kitten to you, hasn't she?'

'Yes, you are right, she has.' Mrs Pickering reached out and lifted up the tiny, bedraggled kitten. 'Isn't it strange – Debbie knew she was dying so she brought her kitten here. And on Christmas Day.'

I bent down and put my hand on Debbie's heart. There was no beat. 'I'm afraid she has died.' I lifted the feather-light body, wrapped it in the piece of sheet and took it out to the car.

When I came back, Mrs Pickering was still stroking the kitten. The tears had dried, and she was bright-eyed as she looked at me.

'I've never had a cat before,' she said.

I smiled. 'Well, it looks as though you've got one now.'

And she certainly had. The kitten grew rapidly into a sleek, handsome and bouncy tabby cat and Mrs Pickering called him Buster. He wasn't timid like his little mother and he lived like a king – and with the ornate collar he always wore, looked like one too.

I watched him grow up with delight, but the occasion that always stays in my mind was the following Christmas Day, a year after his arrival.

I was on my way home after visiting a farmer with a sick cow, and I was looking forward to my Christmas dinner. Mrs Pickering was at her front door when I passed her house and I heard her call out, 'Merry Christmas, Mr Herriot! Come in and have a drink to warm you up.'

I had a little time to spare, so I stopped the car and went in. In the house there was all the festive cheer of last year and the same glorious whiff of sage and onion stuffing. But this year, there was no sorrow – there was Buster!

He was darting up to each of the Basset hounds in turn, ears pricked, eyes twinkling, dabbing a paw at them, and then streaking away.

Mrs Pickering laughed. 'Buster does tease them so. He gives them no peace.'

She was right. For a long time, the dogs had led a rather sedate life: gentle walks with their mistress, plenty of good food, and long snoring sessions on the rugs and armchairs. Then Buster arrived.

He was now dancing up to the youngest dog again, head on one side, asking him to play. When he started boxing with both paws, it was too much for the Basset who rolled over with the cat in a wrestling game.

'Come into the garden,' said Mrs Pickering. 'I want to show you something.'

She lifted a hard rubber ball from the sideboard and we went outside.

She threw the ball across the lawn and Buster bounded after it over the frosty grass, his tabby coat gleaming in the sun. He seized the ball in his mouth, brought it back to his mistress, dropped it at her feet, and waited. Mrs Pickering threw it and again Buster brought it back.

I gasped. A retriever-cat!

The Bassets looked on unimpressed. Nothing would ever make *them* chase a ball, but Buster did it again and again as though he would never tire of it.

Mrs Pickering turned to me. 'Have you ever seen anything like that?'

'No,' I replied. 'He is a most remarkable cat.'

We went back into the house where she held Buster close to her, laughing as the big cat purred loudly. Looking at him, so healthy and contented, I remembered his mother who had carried her tiny kitten to the only place of comfort and warmth that she had ever known.

Mrs Pickering was thinking the same thing because she turned to me and, although she was smiling, her eyes were thoughtful. 'Debbie would be pleased,' she said.

I nodded. 'Yes, she would. It was just a year ago today she brought him in, wasn't it?'

'That's right.' She hugged Buster again. 'The best Christmas present I've ever had.'